CENGAGE Learning

Drama for Students, Volume 8

Staff

Editorial: David M. Galens, *Editor.* Andrea Henry, Mark Milne, and Kathleen Wilson, *Contributing Editors.* James Draper, *Managing Editor.* David Galens, *"For Students" Line Coordinator.*

Research: Victoria B. Cariappa, *Research Manager.* Andrew Guy Malonis, Barbara McNeil, Gary J. Oudersluys, Maureen Richards, and Cheryl L. Warnock, *Research Specialists.* Patricia Tsune Ballard, Wendy K. Festerling, Tamara C. Nott, Tracie A. Richardson, Corrine A. Stocker, and Robert Whaley, *Research Associates.* Phyllis J. Blackman, Tim Lehnerer, and Patricia L. Love, *Research Assistants.*

Permissions: Maria Franklin, *Permissions Manager.* Kimberly F. Smilay, *Permissions Specialist.* Kelly A. Quin, *Permissions Associate.* Sandra K. Gore, *Permissions Assistant.*

Graphic Services: Randy Bassett, *Image Database Supervisor*. Robert Duncan and Michael Logusz, *Imaging Specialists*. Pamela A. Reed, *Imaging Coordinator*. Gary Leach, *Macintosh Artist*.

Product Design: Cynthia Baldwin, *Product Design Manager*. Cover Design: Michelle DiMercurio, *Art Director*. Page Design: Pamela A. E. Galbreath, *Senior Art Director*.

following: unique and original selection, coordination, expression, arrangement, and classification of information. All rights to this publication will be vigorously defended.

© 2000 Gale Group
27500 Drake Rd.
Farmington Hills, MI 48331-3535

This book is printed on acid-free paper that meets the minimum requirements of American National Standard for Information Sciences—Permanence Paper for Printed Library Materials, ANSI Z39.48-1984.

ISBN 0-7876-4082-4
ISSN 1094-9232

Printed in the United States of America
10 9 8 7 6 5 4 3 2 1

All My Sons

Arthur Miller

1947

Introduction

All My Sons, Arthur Miller's first commercially successful play, opened at the Coronet Theatre in New York on January 29, 1947. It ran for 328 performances and garnered important critical acclaim for the dramatist, winning the prestigious New York Drama Critics' Circle Award.

Miller's earlier play, *The Man Who Had All the Luck* (1944), had not done well and had quickly closed; therefore, at the time *All My Sons* opened,

Miller's reputation as a writer was based almost solely on *Focus* (1945), his lauded novel about anti-Semitism.

All My Sons is now regarded as the first of Miller's major plays. The work also greatly helped the career of Elia Kazan, who had first won accolades for his direction of Thornton Wilder's *The Skin of Our Teeth* in 1942 and after directing *All My Sons* would continue to work with the plays of both Miller and Tennessee Williams to produce both legendary stage productions and important films.

In *All My Sons* Miller evidenced the strong influence of both Henrik Ibsen and Greek tragedy, developing a "formula" that he would brilliantly exploit in his next play, *Death of a Salesman* (1949), which many regard as his finest work.

Author Biography

Arthur Miller was born on October 17, 1915, in New York City. He spent his early years in comfortable circumstances, until his father, Isidore, a prosperous manufacturer, lost his wealth in the economic devastation of the Great Depression. After completing high school, Miller had to take a job in a Manhattan warehouse.

He had not been much of a student, but after reading Dostoevsky's great novel *The Brothers Karamazov* he decided that he was destined to become a writer. He had trouble getting into college but was eventually accepted at the University of Michigan, where he began his apprenticeship as a writer and won several student awards for his work.

After college he returned to New York and worked briefly as a radio script writer, then tried his hand at writing for the stage commercially. His first Broadway play, *The Man Who Had All the Luck* (1944), closed after only four performances, but it did win a Theater Guild award and revealed the young writer's potential.

He had more success with *Focus* (1945), a novel dealing with anti-Semitism. In fact, at the time he wrote *All My Sons* (1947), his first dramatic hit, he was better known as a writer of fiction than as a playwright.

All My Sons established Miller's standing as a

bright and extremely talented dramatist. The play had a good run and won Miller his first New York Drama Critics' Circle Award. Even the least favorable commentators recognized the playwright's great promise.

Miller followed *All My Sons* with three of his most critically and commercially successful plays: *Death of Salesman* (1949), *The Crucible* (1953), and A *View from the Bridge* (1955). In these works, Miller attempted to show that tragedy could be written about ordinary people struggling to maintain personal dignity at critical moments in their lives. With these plays, Miller joined Eugene O'Neill and Tennessee Williams in what in the post-World War II years was generally recognized as the great triumvirate of the American theater.

Miller, a political leftist, gained some notoriety in the 1950s when he refused to cooperate with the House Un-American Activities Committee and was held in contempt of Congress. From this experience he found thematic material for one of his most famous and controversial plays, *The Crucible,* which focuses on the Salem Witch Trials of 1692.

After the 1955 production of A *View from the Bridge,* Miller took a nine-year hiatus from play-writing. In the interim, Miller married and divorced the famous actress, Marilyn Monroe. He did adapt one of his stories, *The Misfits* as a screen vehicle for his celebrated wife but did not complete another Broadway play until 1964, when both *After the Fall* and *Incident at Vichy* were produced. The former play, considered Miller's most experimental play, is also his darkest work, with many autobiographical parallels.

His last Broadway success was *The Price,* produced in 1968. After his next play, *The Creation of the World and Other Business* (1972), failed on Broadway, Miller stopped premiering works in New York. He continued to write plays, and enjoyed some success, but nothing that matched that of his earliest works. Many of his later plays were short one-act plays and works comprised of sketches or vignettes.

His greatest triumphs remain *Death of a Salesman* and *The Crucible.* Both have been revived with great success. In 1999, for example, the New York production of *Death of a Salesman* garnered four Tony awards, including one for best revival and one for best direction. At the age of eighty-four, Miller was also presented with a special, lifetime achievement award for his great contributions to the American theater.

Act One

The play opens on a Sunday morning in August and is set in the back yard of the Keller home, located on the outskirts of an unidentified American town, a couple of years after the end of World War II. Joe Keller, who has been reading classified ads in a newspaper, banters pleasantly with his neighbors, Dr. Jim Bayliss and Frank Lubey. He explains that the apple tree had split in half during the night.

It is a source of some concern, for the tree is a memorial for Joe's son, Larry, and its destruction might upset Joe's wife, Kate. Frank refers to it as Larry's tree and notes that August is Larry's birth month. He plans to cast Larry's horoscope, to see if the date on which he was reported missing in action was a favorable or unfavorable day for him.

The men ask after the Kellers' visitor, Ann, the daughter of Joe's former partner, Steve Deever, who once lived in the house now owned by the Baylisses. Sue, Jim's wife, arrives and sends Jim home to talk on the phone with a patient. She is followed by Frank's wife, Lydia, who reports a problem with a toaster.

Joe's son, Chris, comes from the house, and a neighborhood boy, Bert, darts into the yard. Joe amuses Bert in a role-playing game in which Bert is learning to be a police deputy under Joe's authority. He has shown Bert a gun and they pretend that the basement of the house is actually a jail.

After the others leave, Joe and Chris talk about the tree and the fact that Kate was outside when it fell. She has never stopped hoping that Larry will return, still alive. Her failure to accept his death is a major obstacle for Chris, who hopes to marry Ann. Kate can only think of Ann as Larry's girl, and she can not accept a marriage of Chris and Ann without first accepting her son's death. Chris's proposed solution, much to his father's chagrin, is to leave the Keller home and business unless his father helps him make Kate accept Larry's death.

Kate enters and muses over the significance of the fallen tree and Ann's arrival. She also speaks of a dream in which she saw Larry and expresses her belief that the memorial tree should never have been planted. Exasperated, Chris talks of trying to forget Larry. She sends him off to get an aspirin, then tries to wring from Joe an explanation for Ann's visit. She also discloses that if she were to lose faith in her belief that Larry was alive, she would kill herself.

Chris returns with Ann, and a tense confrontation almost immediately begins. Ann pointedly rejects Kate's hope that Larry is still alive. She also divulges that she is unwilling to forgive her father, now in jail, as Joe once was, convicted of providing the Army Air Force with 121 defective cracked cylinder heads. The parts were used in the engines of P-40 fighter planes, twenty-one of which crashed.

Joe, who was later exonerated, attempts to defend his former partner as a confused, somewhat inept "little man" caught in a situation that he did not fully fathom. Ann is unmoved and holds her father responsible for Larry's death. Yet Kate knows the truth: Joe ordered his partner to weld the cracked cylinder heads and hide the defect.

After Joe and Kate leave, Chris confesses his love to Ann, and she ardently confirms her own for him. She is mystified by his long delay in disclosing his feelings, and he explains that it took him a long time to shake free from a guilt he felt for his survival in the war. They are interrupted when Ann is told that her brother, George, is on the phone.

As she exits, Joe and Chris discuss the fact that George is in Columbus, visiting his father in jail. Ann is heard talking on the phone, trying to mollify her angry brother, while Joe speculates as to the possibility that George and Ann may be trying to open the criminal case again. Chris placates Joe, who shrugs off his concern and begins talking of Chris's future and telling him that he will help Chris and Ann make Kate accept their marriage. Ann then comes out to tell them that George is coming to visit that same evening.

Act Two

It is late afternoon on the same day. Kate enters to find Chris sawing up the fallen apple tree.

After telling Chris that Joe is sleeping, she asks Chris to tell Ann to go home with George. She is afraid that Steve Deever's hatred for Joe has infected his children, and she wants them both to leave.

When Ann appears, Kate returns to the house. Ann wants Chris to tell his mother about their marriage plans, and he promises to do so that evening. As he leaves, Sue enters, looking for her husband. She and Ann discuss Ann's marriage plans. Sue encourages her to move away after her marriage. She is bitter towards Chris, who, as Jim's friend, has tried to convince him to pursue work in medical research, a luxury that the Baylisses can not afford.

When Ann defends Chris, Sue suggests that Chris is a phony, given the fact that Chris has greatly benefited from Joe's ruthless and unethical business practices. She also tells Ann that everyone knows that Joe was as guilty as Steve Deever and merely "pulled a fast one to get out of jail."

When Chris returns, Sue goes in the house to see if she can calm Kate down. Ann tells Chris that Sue hates him, and that the people of the community believe that Joe should be in jail. Chris believes in his father's innocence and tells her that he can not put any stock in what the neighbors believe.

Joining them in the backyard, Joe tells the young lovers that he wants to find George a good local job, and then announces that he even wants to hire Steve Deever when he is released from prison. Chris is adamantly opposed, believing that Deever had wrongly implicated his father, and he does not want Joe to give him a job. Joe exits.

Having picked up George at the train station, Jim Bayliss enters quickly from the driveway. Jim warns Chris that George has "blood in his eye," and that Chris should not let him come into the Keller yard. However, Chris welcomes George as a friend, but from George's surly behavior it is soon clear that he is angry.

As a result of visiting his father, he is convinced that Joe knew about the cracked cylinder heads but ordered Deever to ship them anyway, and he is now intent on stopping Ann from marrying Chris. He presents his father's account of the day the cracked cylinder heads were made, but Chris, believing in his father's innocence, tries to make him leave rather than confront Joe and upset his mother.

The tense situation is defused when Kate and Lydia enter the yard. After some amiable recollections are exchanged, Joe enters and asserts that Steve Deever only blames Joe because Steve, unable to face his faults, could never own up to his mistakes. George seems almost at ease, but when Kate makes a critical blunder, inadvertently disclosing that Joe had not been ill in fifteen years, George is once again upset. Joe's alibi was that he had been home with pneumonia when the defective parts were doctored up and shipped out by Deever; George realizes that Joe's alibi was a lie.

Frank Lubey enters with Larry Keller's horoscope, which speculates that Larry is still alive. Kate wants Ann to leave with George and has even packed her bag. Chris tries to make his mother see that Larry is dead, but Kate, knowing the truth about the defective parts, insists that he must be alive. Otherwise, she believes that Joe is responsible for his death.

Finally realizing the truth, Chris angrily confronts his father, who lamely tries to defend his actions as "business." Chris, profoundly hurt and disillusioned, beats furiously on his father's shoulders.

Act Three

It is 2:00 AM of the following morning. Alone, Kate waits for Chris to return. Jim joins her and asks what has happened; he then reveals that he has known about her husband's guilt for some time. He contends that he hopes that Chris will go off to find himself before returning.

Jim exits just as Joe comes in. Kate tells him that Jim knows the truth. Meanwhile, he is concerned about Ann, who has stayed in her room since Chris left. He talks, too, of needing Chris's forgiveness and his intent to take his own life should he not get it.

Ann enters and hesitantly gives Kate a letter that she had received from Larry after Joe and her father were convicted. Chris returns and tells his father that he cannot forgive him. Ann takes the letter from Kate and gives it to Chris, who reads it aloud.

Composed just before Larry's death, it tells of his plan to take his own life in shame over what his father had done. It suddenly becomes clear to Joe that Larry believed that all the fighter pilots who perished in combat were Joe's sons. He then withdraws into the house, and Chris confirms his plan to turn Joe over to the authorities.

Suddenly, a shot is heard from the house. Chris enters the house, presumably to find his father's body. He returns to his mother's arms, dismayed and crying, and she tells him to forget what has happened and live his life.

Characters

Annie

See Ann Deever

Dr. Jim Bayliss

Jim Bayliss is a close friend of Chris Keller. He and his wife Sue bought the house formerly owned by Steve Deever and his family; this makes him a neighbor of the Kellers. Although Jim suspects that Joe is as guilty as his former partner is, he likes the Keller family. He even tries to protect Joe from a confrontation with George Deever.

Sue Bayliss

Sue Bayliss, Jim's wife, reveals that the town knows the truth about Joe Keller, and, unlike her husband, she basically dislikes the family. However, her animus is largely directed against Chris, not Joe. She believes that he knows his father is guilty and has profited from the situation. As a result, she deems him a phony, and she deeply resents his friendship with her husband.

Bert

Bert is a neighborhood boy. He plays with Joe

in the beginning of the play, pretending to be a policeman. Bert's gullibility provides a comic counterpoint to the more serious gullibility of Joe's son, Chris, who believes in his father's innocence. Joe has also shown Bert the gun with which, at the end, he kills himself.

Ann Deever

Ann is the attractive daughter of Steve Deever, Joe's former partner. She is visiting the Kellers for the first time since her boyfriend, Larry Keller, was reported missing in action. She has been invited by Chris; they are in love, much to the consternation of Kate, Chris's mother.

Ann believes that her father is guilty and has refused to visit him in jail. She is perhaps blinded by her love for Chris, whom she plans to marry.

Media Adaptations

- *All My Sons* was adapted as a film in 1948. Chester Erskine wrote the screenplay. Directed by Irving Reis, the cast included Edward G. Robinson as Joe Keller, Burt Lancaster as Chris, Mady Christians as Kate, Louisa Horton as Ann Deever, and Howard Duff as George Deever. The film is available on videocassette.

- The play was also produced as a television play in 1955 and again in 1987. The 1955 version featured Albert Dekker, Patrick McGoohan, and Betta St. John in its cast. It is not, however, extant. The 1987 version, directed by John Power, was a television special produced by the Corporation for Public Broadcasting. It featured Joan Allen, Zeljko Ivanek, Michael Learned, Joanna Miles, Aidan Quinn, Alan Scarfe, Marlow Vella, and James Whitmore. It is not currently available on videocassette.

However, she carries what is in fact a suicide letter that Larry wrote to her before his final mission. Deeply shamed by his father's conviction, Larry disclosed his inability to live with the fact of his father's crime. When Kate continues to refuse to believe that Larry is dead and tries to prevent her marriage to Chris, Ann is forced to show her the letter. With the Larry's final thoughts revealed, Chris is forced to face his father's guilt.

George Deever

George is Steve Deever's son and brother to Ann Deever. He is a lawyer and a threat to Joe Keller, who fears that he might try to reopen the case that put Joe and his father in prison. After visiting his father in jail, he confronts Joe. George is convinced that Joe destroyed his father and was the real instigator of the crime. When he discovers that Ann is in love with Chris, he tries to persuade her to leave with him.

Kate's kindness almost placates him, and he even seems ready to accept Joe's version of what happened; but Kate inadvertently reveals that Joe was not sick when the defective parts were shipped and thereby confirms what his father had told George. He storms off before Chris is forced to face the truth and Joe commits suicide.

Chris Keller

Chris, at age thirty-two, is Joe and Kate Keller's surviving son. He is in love with Ann Deever, the former girlfriend of his deceased brother, Larry. He invites Ann to visit the Keller home so that he might propose to her.

A veteran of World War II, Chris now works for his father, Joe. Since being exonerated and released from prison, Joe has built a very successful company. Chris believes that his father is innocent, as he feels was proved at the pardon hearing before Joe's release. An idealist, he has a very strong sense of justice and responsibility, and he bears a residual guilt for surviving the war when many of his friends died.

He also believes that one should be guided by the noblest principles, and he tries to encourage his friend, Jim Bayliss, to leave his medical practice to pursue a higher calling in medical research. His influence angers Jim's wife, Sue, who believes that Joe is guilty and that Chris is a hypocrite.

Although his love for his father blinds him to the truth, when Joe's guilt is finally revealed, he believes that he has no choice but to see to it that his father is returned to prison.

Joe Keller

The Keller family patriarch, Joe is a self-made businessman who started out as a semi-skilled laborer and worked his way up in the business world to become a successful manufacturer. He owns a factory, where he employs his surviving son, Chris.

Initially, Joe seems like a very genial, good-natured man, almost like a surrogate grandfather to the neighborhood kids. He is very outgoing with his neighbors, and has a disarming tendency to engage in some self-deprecation, noting, among other things, that he is not well educated or as articulate as those around him. It is partly a pose, however, for he actually prides himself on his business acumen. His business means a great deal to him, almost as much as his family.

Unfortunately, Joe has sacrificed quite a bit for such success. During the war, he ordered his partner, Steve Deever, to cover cracks in some airplane-engine parts, disguise the welds, and send them on to be used in fighter planes, causing the death of twenty-one pilots. Although convicted, Joe put the blame on Steve and got out of prison.

When the truth is revealed about Larry's death, Joe is at first unwilling to face the responsibility. Finally realizing the consequences of his actions and his limited course of action, he commits suicide.

Kate Keller

Kate is Joe's wife and the mother of Chris. Although her older son, Larry, was reported missing in action during World War II, she hopes that he has survived and will eventually return home. She hopes for this not only because she loves her son, but also because she knows the truth about Joe: he ordered his partner Steve to cover the cracks in the cylinder heads that eventually resulted in the death of several American fighter pilots. Although Larry never flew a P-40 fighter, Kate believes that Joe must be held accountable as his murderer. She is finally forced to face Larry's death when confronted with the letter that he sent to Ann Deever announcing his impending suicide.

Her motives are hidden from Chris, who earnestly wants her to face the fact of Larry's death and move on with life. He wants to marry Larry's former girl friend, Ann Deever, but he knows he will not be able to obtain his mother's blessing as long as she continues to hold on to her unrealistic conviction that Larry is still alive.

Kate is a sympathetic character. She is kind and motherly, but the truth of her husband's guilt tortures her. As the pressure mounts, she develops physical symptoms of her inner agony. At the end, after Joe shoots himself, she tells Chris to live—something she had not been able to do since the death of her other son.

Frank Lubey

Frank Lubey is Lydia's husband. A haberdasher, he is perceived as flighty and socially inept. Gracious, intelligent, and attractive, Lydia makes him seem rather silly by comparison. Frank, always missing each draft call-up by being a year too old, did not go to war. He married Lydia when George Deever, her former beau, did not return to his hometown from the war.

Frank's foolishness extends to his belief in astrology, which would be harmless enough were it not for the fact that he keeps Kate's hopes of Larry's survival alive with his insistence that Larry's horoscope could reveal the truth.

Lydia Lubey

Lydia is Frank's wife. She is a charming, very pretty woman of twenty-seven, described by Miller as a "robust laughing girl." Before George went off to war, she was his girlfriend; when he did not return home after his father was imprisoned, she married Frank, a dull alternative. When George does come to confront the Kellers with his father's accusations, he is reminded of everything he lost. He also knows that Lydia deserved better than she got.

Mother

See Kate Keller

American Dream

In a sense, *All My Sons* is a critical investigation of the quest to achieve material comfort and an improved social status through hard work and determination. In the Horatio Alger myth, even a disadvantaged, impoverished young man can attain wealth and prestige through personal fortitude, moral integrity, and untiring industry. Joe Keller is that sort of self-made man, one who made his way from blue-collar worker to factory owner. However, Joe sacrifices his integrity to materialism, and he makes a reprehensible decision that sends American pilots to their deaths, something he is finally forced to face.

Atonement and Forgiveness

Paradoxically, Joe Keller's suicide at the end of *All My Sons* is both an act of atonement and an escape from guilt. It stems from Joe's realization that there can be no real forgiveness for what he had done. The alternative is confession and imprisonment. Death offers Joe another alternative.

Forgiveness must come from Kate and Chris. The letter written by Larry reveals that he deliberately destroyed himself during the war, profoundly shamed by his father's brief imprisonment for fraud and profiteering. It is a devastating irony that Joe's initial attempt to do right by his family—resulting in fraud and the deaths of twenty-one fighter pilots—leads to destruction of his world.

Topics for Further Study

- Research the problem of profiteering during both World War II and the Cold War. Was it a prevalent phenomenon? What forms did it take (e.g., cost overruns, ridiculous pricing, fraudulent claims)? Describe the worst case you can find from your research.

- Trace the influence of either Henrik Ibsen or Anton Chekhov on *All My Sons.*

- Investigate Miller's role in the

investigations of the House Un-American Activities Committee (HUAC), including his contempt conviction and eventual exoneration. Do you agree with Miller's position? Give reasons for your answer.

- Determine the influence of the politics of the left, including socialism and communism, on the American theater and cinema during the 1930s and 1940s.

Choices and Consequences

All My Sons employs a pattern that is fundamental to most tragedies. Protagonists in tragedy must, in some degree, be held accountable for their actions. When faced with a moral dilemma, they often make a wrong choice. Joe, at a critical moment, elected to place his family's finances above the lives of courageous American soldiers.

The revelations that lead up to Joe's tragic recognition of guilt and his suicide, the final consequences of his choice, are essential to *All My Sons*. There is a sense of *anake,* or tragic necessity, that moves the work along towards its inevitable moment of truth and awful but final retribution.

Death

The key in the tragic arc of *All My Sons* is Kate

Keller's refusal to accept the death of her son, Larry. Initially, prone to false hopes, it seems that she is in denial; finally, it is revealed that her need to believe that Larry is alive allows her to avoid the terrible consequences of her husband's deeds. She realizes that if Larry is dead, then Joe is responsible for his death—something Larry himself confirmed in his letter to Ann. All along, Kate knew her husband's guilt but desperately avoided it, knowing that it would destroy her family.

Duty and Responsibility

Joe Keller's sense of duty and responsibility is to the material comfort of his family and the success of his business. At a weak moment, under pressure, he puts these values ahead of what should clearly have been a higher duty, his obligation to human life. His fear of losing lucrative government contracts—essentially his greed—blinded him to the murder he was committing.

Ethics

Joe's decision to send defective parts is not merely a result of skewed values, it is a serious breach of ethics. Joe does not fully comprehend how serious a breach it is. To him, success is more important than anything else, including human life and the good of his country. By setting up this ethical situation, Miller clearly questions the implications of a value system that puts material success above moral responsibilities to others.

Guilt and Innocence

In *All My Sons,* there are hints that Joe is troubled by his guilt—even before his eventual suicide. His suspicions of Ann and George Deever reveal his fears of being forced to face the truth. Even when he attempts to atone for his guilt by helping his former partner, Steve Deever as well as Deever's son, George, his offer seems rather lame given the enormity of his guilt. There is no way he can atone for the deaths of the American fighter pilots, however, something that he finally realizes.

Punishment

Joe's death at the end of *All My Sons* is paradoxically both punishment and escape. In one sense, Joe can do no less than pay for his crime with his life. It is not an empty gesture. It is made abundantly clear from the play's beginning that Joe is a man who is full of life and cherishes his roles as both husband and father.

When the truth comes out, Joe has to face not only a return to prison but also the alienation of his remaining son and the destruction his family. Death offers the only escape from that pain. It may also be seen as a sacrificial act, one which saves Joe's son, Chris, from further humiliation.

Revenge

Fueled by his anger over Joe's guilt, George Deever comes to the Keller's house seeking revenge and retribution. He is a major catalyst and intensifies the emotional tension of the play. For a moment, Kate's friendliness and warmth placate him. When, towards the end of the second act, Kate inadvertently confirms the probable truth of his father's accusations, George's anger returns. Joe is then forced to reveal his fraudulent and deceitful actions.

Style

Climax

All My Sons has a very traditional dramatic structure, with carefully orchestrated action that reaches a climax. Although it may be argued that each act has its own climax, with a particularly powerful one in the second act, the final climax occurs in the last act, when Joe finally realizes that he was responsible for the deaths of the American fighter pilots, his "sons."

Conflict

Tension in drama evolves from conflict. In fact, conflict is virtually mandatory in what is termed the dramatic moment, whether in a play or in fiction. A good play generally evinces a sense of a deepening conflict that heightens the emotional tension as the play works towards its climactic moment. Conflict arises as a character strives toward a goal and is met by an obstacle to that goal.

The key conflict in *All My Sons* develops as a result of Chris's desire to marry Ann Deever. Standing in the way of his desire is his mother's ability to block the marriage; she opposes the union because she cannot accept the death of her son, Larry. If she accepts his death, then she must also face Joe's role in it.

Ironically, Chris tries to enlist his father's help in this matter. On account of his love for Ann, Chris pushes his family into facing truths that have tragic and destructive consequences.

Exposition

Exposition in drama is often more of a problem than it is for writers of fiction. Somehow, information about past events and relationships must be conveyed to an audience so that the action in the present can be fully understood. Because *All My Sons* is a realistic play in which all the action occurs on the day in which the family crisis is met and tragically resolved, Miller has few options for revealing Joe's fraudulent past. The action strictly adheres to a normal chronological order, allowing nothing like a flashback or the hallucinatory reveries of the main character so brilliantly used by Miller in his next play, *Death of Salesman.*

Miller's chief device is the reunion, the introduction of a character who needs to be told what has transpired since that character's former estrangement. That character is Ann Deever; inadvertently, she opens old wounds because of her familial relationship with Joe's former partner, Larry. She also bears the truth of Larry's death in a letter that he had written to her. In this way she is like the messenger of Greek tragedy whose task it is to bear in the pain of truth that will force the tragic recognition in the main character.

Foreshadowing

Fore shadowing s of an impending disaster appear in the first act of *All My Sons*. The memorial apple tree planted for Larry is destroyed during a storm in the early morning hours, suggesting a dark force that has the power to destroy the Keller family.

Kate's response to the tree's felling at first seems odd. She says that it should never have been planted in the first place. However, it is soon learned that she has desperately held on to the hope that Larry, reported missing in action during the war, is still alive. That she suffers from the emotional burden of her hope is revealed by her sleeplessness and physical pain.

In its way, even Joe's role-playing game is a foreshadowing. Playing with Bert, they pretend that the Keller home is a jail. This game suggests that Keller views his home as a kind of jail. On account of what he has done, he can not really be free.

Even the play's setting foreshadows events. The backyard of the Kellers is pleasant and, initially, a happy place; but it is also rather insular, hidden from its neighbors by the poplar trees that grow on both sides. The trees stand like sentinels, protecting Joe from the suspicions of his neighbors, most of whom believe that he was at least as guilty as Steve Deever.

Realism

All My Sons strictly adheres to the tenets of realistic drama as first put in practice by such early modern playwrights as Henrik Ibsen and Anton Chekhov. Fundamental to such drama is faithfulness to real life in both character and action. Characters speak and act very much like real people. Nothing happens that could not happen in reality.

However, like the realism of most plays in the Ibsen tradition, the realism of *All My Sons* is of a selective variety, deliberately controlled to advance a particular thesis. Matters are rather conveniently drawn to a climactic head on a single day with the visit of the two Deever siblings, a coincidence that is nevertheless wholly within the realm of plausibility.

Setting

The setting of *All My Sons,* the Keller's backyard in a small Midwestern town shortly after World War II, has a significant role in the play. The setting suggests comfort and isolation from the community. Isolation is necessary because the townspeople suspect the truth about Joe, that he did what he had been convicted of doing during the war. Yet because he is so successful and provides jobs in the community, they do not openly reproach him for it.

Destructive forces threaten the setting. Nature first invades, destroying the apple tree planted in memory of Larry. It is followed by the "messengers," Ann and George. At the end of the play, the yard is engulfed in the darkness of night, the destructive truth that leaves Kate and Chris alone in the grim aftermath of Joe's suicide.

Thesis

All My Sons is a thesis play that focuses on a problem that Arthur Miller believed was eating at the fabric of American democracy: material greed. Miller's protagonist, Joe Keller, is an affable and pleasant man with a strong sense of family loyalty, but his values have been shaped by a prevalent American belief that human success and worth can best be measured by how many things a person owns.

Joe believes that his son's love is based on material concerns. The fact that Chris wants Joe to atone for his crime finally forces him to recognize his guilt.

Tragic Flaw

Joe lets a love of materialism and fear cloud his moral compass. He sets in motion events that have tragic consequences. Joe fears failure in business, as if, somehow, failure would threaten the love and respect of his family. Under pressure, that fear leads him to make an ill-considered decision to put the lives of American pilots at risk by disguising cracked cylinder heads and shipping them to assembly plants.

Unities

In addition to being a realistic play, *All My Sons* has some characteristics of classical drama, notably an adherence to the so-called dramatic unities of time, place, and action. First, it basically observes the Aristotelian notion that the action should all occur within a twenty-four-hour time period. The action opens in the morning and ends in the early hours on the morning of the next day.

Second, the action all occurs in one locale, the backyard of the Keller home. Third, although the action is not continuous, within each of the three acts the action is continuous, and the three acts are arranged chronologically, as is the standard practice in most realistic plays. Breaks between acts are in part used to indicate the passage of time in the play's action.

Historical Context

In March of 1947, President Harry S. Truman presented the Truman Doctrine to the U. S. Congress. The Truman Doctrine was an anti-Communist declaration that would shape American foreign policy for over four decades. With the Cold War heating up, fears of an international communist conspiracy were rapidly growing. The Truman Doctrine was meant to alleviate some of those very fears.

The now infamous House Un-American Activities Committee (HUAC) began its very visible investigations of alleged communist influence in Hollywood, resulting in the jailing and blacklisting of witnesses who refused to cooperate with investigators. The FBI, meanwhile, looked for evidence of communist infiltration in America; for example, they concluded that Frank Capra's classic Christmas film, *It's a Wonderful Life,* was little more than insidious communist propaganda.

To counter the growing spread of communism in Eastern Europe and Asia, the United States took positive steps to help rebuild the war-torn countries of both its allies and its former enemies, including Germany and Japan. On June 5, 1947, Secretary of State George Marshall announced his plan for the economic recovery of Europe. With the Brussels Treaty of March 17, 1948, the Western European Union, the forerunner of the North Atlantic Treaty

Organization (NATO), was formed.

Compare & Contrast

- **1940s:** In the aftermath of World War II, the industrialized world divided into two armed superpowers: the Soviet bloc of communist nations and the Western democracies. In the West, the threat of communism led to suspicion and paranoia at the highest levels of government. Nuclear war seemed imminent.

  Today: The threat of a nuclear war between the Soviet Union and United States dissipated with the economic and political collapse of the Soviet Union in the 1980s. Instead, the threat of terrorism reigns as well as the growing nuclear capabilities of rogue states such as Pakistan, India, Iran, and Iraq.

- **1940s:** The Nuremberg Trials for war crimes and atrocities, which began soon after World War II, continued into 1949. The trials resulted in the imprisonment or execution of many high-ranking Nazis, particularly those involved in the running the concentration camps, which exterminated millions of victims.

Today: Reaction to genocide in several countries has led to a new call for tribunals to indict and condemn war criminals. A notable example of a modern war criminal is Serbian president Slobodan Milosevic, who in 1999 was charged with the mass murder of ethnic Albanians and indicted by the World Court. Such "ethnic cleansing" has also occurred in other states, including Iraq, Burundi, and Rwanda.

- **1940s:** In the wake of World War II, concerns about wartime profiteering and unethical practices were widespread. In the 1950s such concerns would eventually compel President Dwight D. Eisenhower to warn America about what he called "the industrial-military complex." War profits also took the form of stealing the assets of the war's victims.

Today: In light of charges by several Jewish families that Swiss banks cooperated with Nazis during World War II and expropriated gold stolen from war victims, the whole issue of wartime profiteering has once more emerged. New concerns have emerged over the role some American industrialists may have played in the rise of Germany's military in the 1930s.

- **1940s:** Professional sports, with some rare exceptions (boxing, for example) were largely segregated. It was not until 1947 that the color line in Major League baseball was broken when Jackie Robinson joined the Brooklyn Dodgers of the National League. Until that time, African Americans could play only in the segregated Negro League.

  Today: African Americans successfully compete in professional sports that seemed almost the exclusive domain of white athletes, notably tennis and golf.

Meanwhile, King Michael of Romania abdicated, bringing another European country into the Soviet bloc. India and Pakistan were granted independence from Great Britain. In that same year, Mother Teresa left her Loreto order to move into the slums of Calcutta to establish her first school.

In Roswell, New Mexico, in July, 1947, there was a rash of UFO sightings and the reported crash of an alien space ship, the basis for what many still consider a lame government cover-up of the truth. Also that summer, Jackie Robinson, the first

African American baseball player to play in the Major Leagues, had joined the Brooklyn Dodgers and was on his way to winning the National League Rookie of the Year award.

In cinema, Elia Kazan, the director of *All My Sons,* won an Oscar for his direction of *Gentlemen's Agreement,* a film about anti-Semitism. Chuck Yeager became the first human to break the sound barrier in October, 1947. Breaking a different kind of barrier, Bell Telephone Laboratories introduced the transistor, the first important Postwar breakthrough in the evolution of microelectronics, fundamental in the development of the post-industrial, information-age technology of the late twentieth century.

Critical Overview

All My Sons was Arthur Miller's first successful play on Broadway. In hindsight, it may seem that the work lacks the great imaginative force of his next play, *Death of Salesman* (1949), still widely regarded as his masterpiece, but in *All My Sons* Miller certainly showed that he could both use dialogue very well and construct a riveting drama in the tradition of social realism.

Miller was fortunate to have as his director Elia Kazan, whose mercurial career was then rapidly rising, and an excellent cast, headed by Ed Begley as Joe Keller, Beth Merrill as Kate, Arthur Kennedy as Chris, Lois Wheeler as Ann Deever, and Karl Maiden as her brother, George. In most reviews, the quality of the production was recognized and applauded. The play chalked up a run of 328 performances and garnered the New York Drama Critics' Circle Award. It was an impressive achievement for a new and virtually unknown playwright.

The work did not receive uniform raves, but it did win the approval of some influential critics, notably Brooks Atkinson of the *The New York Times,* the city's most distinguished newspaper. In his autobiography, *Timebends* Miller says "it was Brooks Atkinson's campaign for *All My Sons* that was responsible for its long run and my recognition as a playwright."

Among other things, Atkinson defended the play against those who took umbrage with Miller's depiction of an American businessman as one who puts material comfort and success above moral responsibility. For Atkinson, the play was "the most talented work by a new author in some time," and though he recognized the important contribution of Kazan and the cast to the play's power, he credited Miller with devising a "pitiless analysis of characters that gathers momentum all evening and concludes with both logic and dramatic impact."

Most reviewers recognized Miller's great promise even while finding flaws in the work. For Joseph Wood Krutch, the plot of the drama was "almost too neat." "The pieces," Krutch argued, "fit together with the artificial, interlocking perfection of a jig-saw puzzle, and toward the end one begins to feel a little uncomfortable to find all the implicit ironies so patly illustrated and poetic justice working with such mechanical perfection." Moreover, Krutch took issue with Miller's "warm respect for all the leftist pieties" and complained that the playwright's "intellectual convictions" are "more stereotyped than his dramatic imagination."

That Miller imposed a classical structure on a social problem play in the tradition of Henrik Ibsen and Anton Chekhov was recognized by his reviewers, whether leftist in sympathies, like Atkinson, or conservative, like Krutch. The influence of both Ibsen and Chekhov is noted by John Mason Brown, who views Dr. Bayliss as a Chekhovian interloper, and in the "spiritual stripteasing" of his main character, the use of symbolism, and his digging into the past to reveal the present and "rush forward to a new climax" the abiding and persistent influence of Ibsen.

To some critics, *All My Sons* also reflected the influence of classical tragedy. In the play, Kappo Phelan wrote, Miller "attempted and delivered a tragedy," and the play is, in fact, the playwright's first successful attempt to create what he would later call "a tragedy of the common man." There are clear parallels to such Sophoclean tragedies as *Oedipus Rex,* both in structure and technique.

Both leftist ideology and the classical influence would keep *All My Sons* in the limelight until *Death of a Salesman* replaced it as the cynosure of critical attention. With that play, Miller came as close as any playwright before or since to demonstrate the validity of his assertion that tragedy is possible in a modern, egalitarian democracy. For that play, as well as *The Crucible* and *View from the Bridge, All My Sons* provided a firm foundation in both its theme of guilt and expiation and its tragic elements and structure.

Sources

Atkinson, Brooks. "The Play in Review," *New York Times,* January 30, 1947, p. 21.

Atkinson, Brooks. "Welcome Stranger," *New York Times,* February 9, 1947, sec. 2, p. 1.

Boggs, W. Arthur. "Oedipus and *All My Sons"* in the *Personalist,* Vol. 42, 1961, pp. 555-60.

Brown, John Mason. "New Talents and Arthur Miller," *Saturday Review of Literature,* Vol. 30, March 1, 1947, pp. 22-4.

Hewes, Henry. "Introduction" in *Famous American Plays of the 1940s.* Dell Publishing, 1960, p. 15.

Hogan, Robert. *Arthur Miller,* University of Minnesota Press, 1964, p. 17.

Klapp, Orrin E. "Tragedy and the American Climate of Opinion," in *Tragedy: Vision and Form,* edited by Robert W. Corrigan, 2nd edition. Harper & Row, 1981, pp. 252-62.

Krutch, Joseph Wood. "Drama," *Nation,* Vol. 164, February 15, 1947, pp. 191,193.

Krutch, Joseph Wood. "The Tragic Fallacy," in *Tragedy: Vision and Form,* edited by Robert W. Corrigan, 2nd edition. Harper & Row, 1981, pp. 227-37.

Miller, Arthur. "Tragedy and the Common Man," in *Tragedy: Vision and Form,* edited by Robert W.

Corrigan, 2nd edition. Harper & Row, 1981, pp. 168-70.

Miller, Arthur. *Timebends: A Life,* Grove Press, 1987, p. 138.

Phelan, Kappo. "The Stage and Screen: *All My Sons,*" *Commonweal,* Vol. 45, February 14, 1947, pp. 445-46.

Further Reading

Adam, Julie. *Versions of Heroism in Modern American Drama: Redefinitions by Miller, Williams, O'Neill and Anderson,* St. Martin's Press, 1991.

> Examining and comparing the protagonists of major American playwrights who attempted to write tragedy, Adam finds that their heroism can fit into distinct categories: idealism, martyrdom, self-reflection, and survival.

Gross, Barry. "*All My Sons* and the Larger Context," *Modern Drama,* Vol. 18, 1975, pp. 15-27.

> Gross examines Joe Keller and his son Chris in light of Miller's aim to create a play functioning as "legislation," exhibiting a strong social purpose, and examines the generation gap between the father and son.

Hayman, Ronald. *Arthur Miller,* Frederick Ungar Publishing, 1972.

> In this brief monograph, Hayman offers a good critical introduction to Miller's earliest plays. Hayman, concludes that Miller's principal concern is with cause and effect.

Hogan, Robert. *Arthur Miller,* University of Minnesota Press, 1964.

> A brief work in the pamphlet series on American writers, Hogan's study is a critical overview of Miller's early works up to and including *After the Fall.* It notes the similarity of structure between *All My Sons* and *Oedipus Rex.*

Miller, Arthur. *Timebends: A Life,* Grove Press, 1987.

> Miller's autobiography offers insights to all his work written into the 1980s. He offers personal reflections on his plays.

Moss, Leonard. *Arthur Miller,* Twayne Publishers, 1967.

> Moss examines Miller's "technical resources," his "dialogue styles, narrative conventions, symbolic devices, and structural principles."

Moss, Leonard. "Arthur Miller and the Common Man's Language," *Modern Drama,* 7 (1964), pp. 52-9.

> Moss's article explores Miller's tendency to use ordinary speech for the expression of ethical abstractions. It uses *All My Sons* to illustrate some of its points.

Wells, Arvin R. "The Living and the Dead in *All My*

Sons," Modern Drama, Vol. 7, 1964, pp. 46-51.

This article argues that *All My Sons* and other Miller plays have a "density of texture" that is much greater than that of a "typical social thesis play."

.

Lightning Source UK Ltd.
Milton Keynes UK
UKHW02f2108220218
318351UK00011BA/498/P